sunsets & tangerines

P.S.

Copyright © 2020 Paola Mondardo Sartori

All rights reserved

No part of this book may be reproduced, or stored in a retrieval system, or transmitted in
any form or by any means, electronic, mechanical, photocopying, recording, or otherwise,
without express written permission of the publisher.

ISBN 9798554420085

Cover design by: Tomaz Saavedra

Editorial board: Andrezza T. Postay

Printed in the United States of America

To the younger me.
I just wish I could tell you it will get better.

contents

cracks • 9

sunsets • 39

mirrors • 71

tangerines • 103

Preface

It's funny how writing a preface seems more challenging to me than writing this book. Perhaps because what you are going to read here came out of me almost as a reaction, almost as automatic as tears on a rainy day or smiles on starry nights.

On the other hand, writing a preface requires me to sit down and deliberately start talking about myself and what these words here mean to me. About how I clung to them in such a desperate way when I had nothing else to hold on to. Or about how they came out of my fingers like serenades when I managed to learn to lessen the pain by piling laughter on top of tangerines.

2019 was a difficult year for me. And I use the word difficult because perhaps the other words that would describe this year are too heavy for a preface. But still, the year of my 28 years changed me a lot. And I wanted to remember. I wanted to remember the 365 sunsets that brought me to 29. So I made them all into this book. I hope you like it.

P.S.

cracks

P.S.

the beginning

the beginning is like a drug
it makes you high and then makes you down
then it consumes you until you are craving for more
the beginning is full of wondering
and it's all you can think about
even when you're trying not to
the beginning doesn't demand reality
doesn't make you feel the weight
of all the choices you've ever made
it's just a mask with all your good sides
and the projections of all the good endings
the beginning is like a drug, it's addictive
in a way you don't even realize
but then you are sober
and the beginning is full of lies.

P.S.

silence

i keep it silent
although i have two hundred and four words to say to you
'cause i know who we are
and i know who we'll be
after these words slip through my mouth
and i don't want to lose you
and i don't want to lose myself
so i keep it silent
'til one day i have the courage to say it.

P.S.

P.S.

it's not you, it's me

i came to you
so many times
begging so badly
for you to change me
that i couldn't see
i was asking you
for the only thing
you couldn't do for me.

P.S.

sunsets & tangerines

do you stop or do i?

we keep ourselves in this dance
as if each step would bring us closer
to what we really want
we look each other in the eye
just not to pay attention to our feet
that clumsily step on each other
in a vain attempt
to set the pace right
do you stop or do i?

P.S.

P.S.

lost not found

we lost each other's happiness
we keep looking desperately
in corners and drawers of ourselves
it's gone
it hurts so badly we cannot breathe
'cause we lost each other's happiness,
but we kept each other's souls.

P.S.

broken pieces

my desperate eyes envy your focused and calm soul

in the middle of this nonstop storm

that happens in my head

i try to find comfort in the way you look at me

and it hurts when i realize

that you are always picking up my pieces,

trying to reassemble that girl that you fell for.

P.S.

P.S.

go away

(but hold me tight).

P.S.

sunsets & tangerines

but i believed in you

you said
you would never lie to me
as if that wasn't
the biggest one of them.

P.S.

september

of all the millions and thousands of ways
i imagined us falling apart
this was never one of them
and maybe that's why it happened.

P.S.

reality hurts

it tastes a little bit bitter

when i hear their names spilling from your lips

and i keep trying to understand

what exactly i am feeling

but all i can do is find out what i'm not

i'm not feeling special as i imagined i would

the way all Hollywood movies made me believe that i should

so i face that reality is not good enough

it's much too real and there is no crazy passion

there is no exchange of glances in the crowd

and fights with kisses in the rain

or uncontrollable desires that make you give in

before you can even take off your shoes

there is just me

and there is just you

spilling names on a drunk night.

P.S.

utopia

i want you to love me the way i dreamed.

P.S.

sunsets & tangerines

pretty little lies

tell me you love me
like you never loved and never will
tell me you'll run away with me and wake up in Tokyo
just so we could get drunk and watch the sun rise again
draw patterns on my skin
and tell me it's just to make me smile
and not because you want to find forgiveness
tell me that you'll follow me
until your feet hurt and you heart sinks
and you feel like you're underwater unable to breathe
keep telling me
these pretty little lies
so that i can feed on them
and make them poetry.

P.S.

P.S.

winter & tangerines

i open my eyes lazily
while my hands blindly search
for the long-missing blanket
in this cold bed
that was once so warm
when i finally find it
burying my body in it like a little child
i smell the tangerines
almost fading away
from the left side pillow
the one you chose
because you couldn't handle windows
and as i breathe you into me
i feel afraid
afraid that one day i will wake up
and the tangerines will finally be gone
and all that i'm gonna feel
is this cold breeze
reminding me cruelly
of all that i had
and all that i lost.

P.S.

decalcomania

i merged with your shadow
without even noticing
i breathed your air through my mouth
'til i made it mine
after some time
when i looked at my reflection
searching for light brown eyes
i found dark ones staring back at me
and that's when i realized
that i would kill myself slowly
just to feel what it's like to be you.

P.S.

P.S.

you love me

i can believe in your love for my surface,
but i'm damn sure you wouldn't want to dive.

P.S.

untitled 6

you asked me if i still think about us
i let the sounds of traffic
take the place of my voice
'cause i was so afraid to let you know
that despite all this time
i still haven't learned how to stop doing it.

P.S.

P.S.

if i wanted more
would you let me have it?

P.S.

sunsets & tangerines

say it again

that thing you said
that ate me inside
and made me sink in
'til i couldn't see the shallow
did you know how sharp it was?
did you know how deep it would cut?
and yet you decided to release it on me?

P.S.

P.S.

just make me stay

you chose to hate me
just so you can forget that you loved me once
but although you devote yourself to blue memories
and try to believe that we were always off-key
you can see in my sore eyes
that i will never be able to remove you from my body
'cause even though it was me who chose to walk away
you never tried to make me stay.

P.S.

i would sing songs about us

i would sing every single word
and let them float together
'til they built up your face
i would cling to the happy notes
twist my feet, take a spin
and dance to the beat
i would feel an itch in my chest
and then the urge to scream
that nobody's gonna love you better
i would let smiles creep past my lips
as my mind imagined us kissing each other
on the top of burning cities
i would...
if it still didn't hurt.

P.S.

P.S.

one plus one makes two

we are not one
i am fire and explosions
and a dance between orange and yellow
and you are an entire ocean
so calm and so angry and so heavy
we can coexist together brilliantly
launching fireworks
and warm breaths
and refreshing bodies
with the music of countless waves
but we cannot be one
because if you keep trying
to make me be an ocean
i will disappear into a mountain
of white and tearful smoke
and all that will be left
is a silent dark blue depth.

P.S.

déjà vu

we can climb a thousand mountains
but we'll still be us
time will make us tired
and maybe just a little bitter
we can try to pretend we have changed
and make ourselves believe that we have evolved
learning from every rock that hit our heads
(and made everything dizzy)
but darling
the sad truth is
we'll still be us.

P.S.

P.S.

the end

i'm sorry that it had to be this way
and i know you're sorry too
but the universe doesn't care
the end will not be me and you.

P.S.

lawful good

these values

you hold until your knuckles turn white

as if they are what keep us together

they are responsible

for the suffocating feeling

that keeps me from sleeping

you need to understand

before it's too late

that they will not keep us together

they will tear us apart.

P.S.

there is no such thing as fairy tales

love is not enough
never was
so even if we fall apart
and exchange glances in the crowd
pretending we don't know each other's faces
it's still gonna hurt
'cause i'm still gonna love you
but i'll keep walking
and so will you.

P.S.

sunsets & tangerines

two minutes to midnight

how many times have i cried for you?
should i have counted?
would that make it more meaningful?
or would it make me realize
what i'm desperately trying not to see?

P.S.

P.S.

blue sweater

if i close my eyes tightly
for seven full seconds
i can feel your body on my skin
and then
when i'm almost tired of seeing black
i can see that kitchen again
but my glass is already empty
although my mouth is still busy
and i can't find my blue wool sweater
just the shivers given to me by the cold winter wind
(hitting my warm chest and making me feel real)
yet the window looks just the same
sleepy and shining
carrying all the weight of being an illusion
and with these utopian sensations in my mind
i decide to open my eyes and get away
'cause this time i have no reason to leave
but i also found no reason to stay.

P.S.

untitled 4

sometimes it's better to let go
do it for you
let it go.

P.S.

sunsets

P.S.

when did it happen?

when did everything stop being enough?

P.S.

cabaret

i feel the beat
all over my body
it pauses and hits me again
every two and a half seconds
but it's enough to make me self-conscious
about the blood that runs through my veins
so i close my eyes
and breathe in the warm air
that touches all the sweaty bodies
dancing on the floor
and when i open them again
tasting the whiskey on my tongue
and filled with all the different colors
that somehow manage to lock me in place
i can truly see them
lost in youth and high as heaven
it makes me remember
of what they're all trying to forget
so i ask the bartender for another shot
grab my jacket
and leave.

P.S.

P.S.

panic attack

everything is fine

people are laughing and dancing

even though they don't really understand why

the sounds of joyful screams run through the air

and reach the bottom of my stomach making it twist

everything is fine

step by step, bounce by bounce

bodies find their way into lusty eyes

and there are hugs and confessions

and the taste of alcohol

everything is fine

but heavy

and the bathroom door calls my name

as if it were freedom

so i lock myself in for a moment

just for a breather

everything is fine

and suddenly the air is too damn hot

and i'm crawling outside

'cause i need to look at the sky

i take a deep breath

everything is fine

these are the best years of your life

they are all here

the ones you carry as a first aid case

but somehow it seems too much

sunsets & tangerines

it's just too much
it's too damn much
everything is fine.

P.S.

P.S.

city lights

i hate this fucking city
still, i find myself sitting on the balcony
deeply looking at her
searching among her lights
memorizing the way the pretty colors of the sunset
touch her borders
(like i could never do)
i keep staring at her
as if i'm challenging her to make a move
use her pawns and strike again
when i look at the buildings and the countless windows
i suddenly can see all the places where i'm not
and all the lives that are not mine
and my body gets taut
when i realize that i'm stuck here
with all these lights
and all this suffering
'cause i know i'll never be able to strike back.

P.S.

the things that i feel

the pain in my eyes
the way i feel them burn
every time i crash
every time it overflows
and i lose the control
that i was holding so carefully.

P.S.

hometown

it's been eleven years
and everything is entirely the same
but different
i changed so much
and even though the buildings have exactly the same colors
my eyes don't capture them like they did before
and what i once thought would mean the world to me
today is just a distant memory
a remnant between the blur of a thousand tears
and a hundred laughs
during a time when my whole life seemed to fit only here
'til one day it didn't.

P.S.

mom & dad

i'm sorry i lied
i guess you don't realize how deeply i'm broken
but you know that something is wrong
nevertheless, when i say i'm alright,
that i'm just running after the millions of things
i have to do at work
you try just once
asking if i'm really fine
if the problem is just the time
and when i whisper a yes trying to say a no
you say it's ok, that it's just a phase
and it will pass
it makes me feel guilt
lying to you
but i have no other option
you couldn't handle the truth.

P.S.

P.S.

time

all stars
eventually die
all they can do about it
is to shine the brightest
until they beautifully fade away.

P.S.

19' carnival

i went there
far away from home
walked through the colored lights
got high between the ups and downs
of long staircases and pretty faces
'cause i needed to find
a reason to go back
but all i could find out
was why i needed to stay.

P.S.

P.S.

are you happy now?

so are you happy now?
now that you managed to get out of that damn city?
now that you've conquered your independence
and made it all about you?
are you finally happy
after all these years?
or did you realize once and for all
that there is no such thing as happiness
there are only ups and downs
and you in-between?

P.S.

nameless

isn't it weird when you can't describe a feeling?

you try to use the words someone once taught you

but none of them fit its shape

you say it's heavy, but not only that

you say it's cold, but it's not even close yet

and then you try to make analogies

like when you were a kid and tried to climb a tree

but you stepped on the wrong branch and almost fell

so your heart ached for more than a second

'cause you met fear for the first time

or when you dived into that pool

that was a few feet taller than you

and while you were trying to swim to the top

your lungs started to burn

and you wondered if you were going to die like that

but it still doesn't seem enough

you can't completely relate it to what you're feeling

it just fucking hurts

it just makes you nauseous

and you feel like you need to find out

you have to name it

you have to name it so you can send it away

but you can't

so you cry.

P.S.

P.S.

loneliness is a fucking bitch

this is the thing about loneliness
it doesn't show up only when you're by yourself
it does not wait when it's dark and cold
and your apartment is so empty
that you can hear all the city sounds through your window
the thing about loneliness is that it's always there
even when somebody is hugging you or telling you a good joke
it's there when you are at parties
dancing and sweating and kissing pretty boys
it's there when you are visiting your parents
and they keep telling you how much they miss you
and how you need to come more often
it's there, squeezing your chest
when the one you swore to love
takes you by the hand and says he wants to marry you
it's always there
like a shadow
walking beside you
telling you that no one knows
that no one truly understands what you feel
that only you can sense the hollow
only you
and no one else
loneliness is a fucking bitch.

P.S.

cliché

it's always one day after another
such a cliché
and it makes you feel kind of numb
when you realize that all the good ones
only happened 'cause you were distracted
so you repeat like a prayer to yourself
"do not think about it too much"
you focus on the lips of the strangers
they talk like everything was perfect and shines
and you count every single drop of rain
that falls from your umbrella
and hits your shoes making you feel wet
just to fill yourself
with the meaninglessness of the world
'cause you know
that if you dare, just once, to perceive
the empty indifference of the universe,
you're gonna embrace this emptiness
'til you make it yours.

P.S.

humanity

nobody told me
that being human
was gonna be
this constant feeling of lack.

P.S.

how does it taste to you?

it tastes like fear
but at the same time
it goes down my throat
burning like relief
on some days it's like a million cuts
on others like seesaws at midnight
but when it touches my lips
with the bitter taste of not being enough
i know the next day it will come back
as the taste of giving up.

P.S.

heavy

that's enough
there is only so many rocks
i can carry
before i drown.

P.S.

wednesday

i wanna get drunk
but i don't
i wish i could stop drowning in it
that i would not crave the numb sensation
that makes me forget existence every time that it hurts
i wish i could see the world without sad eyes
and truly enjoy it
with smiles and giggles
and not with this constant feeling that it's all a big lie
i wish i could try you without whiskey on my tongue
really try you, really be there and really feel
but i can't
so i ask for more ice
and i drown myself in.

P.S.

P.S.

moving

while i sweep away all the papers
that once contained the blood and sweat of my youth
i face this bitter feeling
of realizing that time has passed
that my dreams have changed
that i grew old
and finally acknowledged what life really is
but with this wave of odd emotions
i can't help but miss those weird years
not because i was younger
not because i was happier
but because i was so blissfully ignorant.

P.S.

keep it on repeat

i will find someone different than you
but she's gonna look at me the same way
i know, because the first time i knocked on your door
i was running away from old memories
of a city that i once loved too.

P.S.

untitled 5

i don't understand why
this city keeps looking at me
staring at me full of dreams
as if i had something to give her
... i have nothing left.

P.S.

death

it's an irrational thing
to fear the inevitable
and yet
we do.

P.S.

P.S.

author

i guess at some point
everyone gets tired
of meticulously scratching the lines
that form all the sad words.

P.S.

untitled 1

there is a void
echoing in my chest
making me swallow hard
even with my lips so dry
that catches me off guard
and makes me feel weak
it penetrates my skin
and makes my shoulders heavy
... i just wish i could name it.

P.S.

the culprit

doctor says i'm sad because i need some pills
mom says i'm sad because i don't believe in god
he says i'm sad because he's not enough for me
everyone tries to find something to blame
'cause it's too scary to accept
i'm sad because i'm being me.

P.S.

hide and seek

they gave me a choice

i could choose pain

or i could choose nothing at all

i decided i couldn't take the silence

i like it out loud even when my head is spinning

since then i've been playing hide and seek

some days i find my fears

and it hurts

but some days i close my eyes

and blindly run with a smile plastered on my face.

P.S.

P.S.

following comets

while i'm lying on wet grass
looking at the night sky
as if trying to get a sarcastic answer
from the universe
it's a question to myself
that keeps tingling in my mind
why do you do this to yourself?
why do you always search for suffering
among the stars?

P.S.

night sky

do you also look up at the starry sky
and feel like crying?
sense the heaviness of the entire universe
pressing on your chest
'til it sinks so deep that it weighs?
have you ever imagined all the stars
and planets and explosions
and suddenly felt alone?
and insignificant?
it took me a few years to understand
while i kept searching in this dark blue void
this strangeness that takes control of your body
is just the feeling of what it's like to be human.

P.S.

P.S.

aftermath

one day
i wish i could look back
and realize it was worth it.

P.S.

mirrors

october, 29

365 days have passed
and when i stop and think
about where i was the last october
i laugh with sad eyes
remembering that silly girl
'cause now it feels so innocent
the way she understood life
and i can't help but wonder
what the next year's girl will think of me now
i just hope she can forgive the chaos.

P.S.

kaleidoscope

i'm stomach butterflies
for those who chose to see me dancing
i'm nightmares and screams
for those who chose to see my inconstancy
and i'm just another fucked up girl
riding bikes through the streets
as if they were motorcycles
for those who chose
not to pay attention to my eyes
it's me, every time
i give the same of me
to each one of them
and it's their choice
never mine
which version of me
they want for themselves
so i'll keep dancing
inconsistently on my motorcycle
arousing butterflies
and nightmares and indifference
wherever i go
it's the only thing i can do
i can only be me.

P.S.

P.S.

wrong

nothing fits
everything bothers them
and when i try to adjust
doesn't feel like me
my mind is a wreck
and my body is a threat
neither one pleases you
and it's always like i'm in the wrong place
keeping myself away from mirrors
not because they can cut
but because i'm afraid of the hollow they carry
i'm tired of the fight
i really am
i truly wish i was a normal girl
but i'm just me
always picking up pieces
and building up mazes
so no one can see.

P.S.

collector

every time i perceive that i can't
something dies inside of me
still, i start collecting
all these little things that i can't do
i keep them in a tiny box
then i separate a drawer
and before i realize i'm drowning
in a room full of little fragments that weigh like iron
i struggle trying to find a way out
but only for three seconds
then i let it be
i let myself die
in my inabilities.

P.S.

P.S.

half a cup of tea

one day i realized
i can't finish anything i start
i drink a cup of tea
but only halfway
i sing melodies to the walls
but only until i start hitting some right notes
one day i want to be a painter
and another day i try to memorize
all the historical periods
that humanity has ever lived
just so that next one i decide
that i should definitely try to run a marathon
it makes me wonder
if i'm really a perfect blur of chaos
or if i'm just scared of what might happen
if one day i make it to the end.

P. S.

the versions of me

stop being disappointed

by a version of me

that lives in your head

there is only one of me

she is here

you can accept her or you can leave

but don't assign her a fault

that is not hers to bear.

P.S.

P.S.

i want it all

can you make me settle down?
i want to stop searching between the windows
i want to look at my feet and smile
facing the shadows i received from the universe
i'm so sick of wanting more
and so tired of running with nowhere to go
can you do this for me?
can you stop me from wanting it all?

P.S.

you're so innocent

you see, you're lonely just like me
(even though you don't believe it)
you keep breathing in this hypnotic rhythm
and drinking your fancy glass of wine
oblivious to the fact that the world will never be enough
while i make all the tables turn
and let my pain overflow like shots of vodka
knowing the fantasies i created are real enough to destroy me
it makes you believe that you're different from me
it makes you think you're safe
but darling,
while i'm suffering out loud
you are suffering in mute
and there is nothing more dangerous
than still having something to lose.

P.S.

i got anger

it takes two and a half seconds
for something to ignite inside of me
burn my skin like it was violins
and spread the heat to all the pieces of you
then, before you know it,
it starts a fire
that consumes you
and turns you into ashes
...'til i'm all alone again.

P.S.

revolution

you spill the word rage
with such disgust
as if it were a demon
you keep repeating
to your surroundings
all the reasons why being angry
must be forbidden and condemned
you don't seem to realize
that rage evokes revolution
and when it burns
it's always for a reason
so let it be, let rage rise
let rage embrace the youth
and those who have been angry for so long
that they have forgotten
what it's like not to feel heavy
let rage speak loudly
let rage be heard
let rage make changes.

P.S.

P.S.

kissed by fire

when i was a little kid
i liked to strike matches
just so i could watch them burn
the sight of everything disappearing
into small incandescent fragments
has always hypnotized me
back there i wished i could be like fire
so they would look at me
creating fragments as i passed
with those same astonished eyes
that the little me looked at matches with
as if i were a goddess
i was so innocent at that time
'cause i couldn't realize
that when humans see gods
they are so afraid of their power
that all they can hope for
is to see them die.

P.S.

sunset in the city

i don't think you will ever understand
why i keep going back to that view
every night and every dawn
but that's okay, 'cause no one ever will.

P.S.

P.S.

storm gods

one two three
i hear them falling from the sky
four five six
suddenly they got angry and i lost count
one billion two billion three billion
now i don't know exactly where to look
and it somehow weighs
four billion five billion and stop
maybe they are not mad anymore
maybe they understood why i did it.

P.S.

routine

i am compulsive

i've been compulsive my whole life

i wake up and i drink too much coffee

just because i always need something to hold

so i drink it 'til my stomach hurts

then i drown myself in old books

only i can't read two pages

'cause two pages become two hundred

and it's already dusk and the city has started to sleep

so i cling on to alcohol

that's 'cause i can't think

surrounded by all the buzz that comes with it

and it makes my muscles finally relax

until it becomes a really bad decision

and i wake up empty and my whole body hurts

(not only my chest)

so i devote myself to feel

and i'm compulsive for feeling as well

thus i bury my mind in tons of warm blankets and sad songs

and i take in every single feeling that pops in my head

'til i'm feeling miserable

so i stand up

and i walk to the kitchen

'cause now i really need a cup of coffee.

P.S.

P.S.

being inside

they say
we need to connect to ourselves
but they don't know
how out of range my mind can be.

P.S.

queen of arms

if i could forget them, i wouldn't
they made me
they are responsible for every little scar
that i proudly expose on my body
from my feet
which once did not have the strength to walk
for a whole damn week
to my mouth
which can perfectly spell all the names
of those who shouldn't have touched it like they did
but i wouldn't have done it differently
'cause while i was supposed to be lying
wounded on the floor
i took all the knives they placed on my heart
melted them down
and built an army for myself.

P.S.

untitled 2

i thought it was you who was holding up your shields
yet somehow i found out it was me
'cause even though i didn't notice
i was building up fortresses inside myself,
locking the gates, so they would remain perfectly stable
and i wouldn't have to collect every single piece of me
displayed on the floor
but it turns out there was no need for someone to break me
i can wonderfully destroy myself alone.

P.S.

elephants

i grew up loving elephants
i envied their calmness and patience
and the way they didn't care about time
i grew up imagining myself among them
the way everything would move in slow motion
as if the wind didn't want me to be distracted
so i drew them everywhere
even though i didn't know exactly
how to trace the lines that would form a trunk
and i spent years wondering if their minds were truly so quiet
that they could hear nature without needing to focus
i grew up loving elephants
and as i was growing up
i realized that this was a resentful kind of love
'cause while i devoted my heart to elephants
i kept wondering if i too could get my fury to stop.

P.S.

black & white

i know i'm hard to approach
i know i don't make it easy for them
but believe me when i say
that i collect people to die for
i am not friendly
but it's because i can't see gray
it's just a deep black and a blinding white
so either i turn my back to the dark
or i feel hypnotized by the light
and i swear
when i finally see light,
i give myself to it 'til there's nothing left.

P.S.

the cold of june

you ask me why i take off my coat
and open the window late at night
letting the cold in
while i look at the streets
it's not a comfortable feeling, i know
it actually makes me shiver
and bothers me
as if something isn't right
but i do it anyway
do you know why?
because the cold breeze
running through my body
raising up every single hair
on the back of my neck
and making everything
so uncomfortable
is a reminder to myself
that i can still feel something
that i can still feel real
that i'm still alive.

P.S.

P.S.

traveler

i belong to all places
but to none of them
every time i get flooded by a sunset
my stomach tingles at the thought of the next one
i guess i'm condemned to walk forever
on streets that i will not remember the name of
hoping that one day
i will find a place that will make me want to stay
and waiting impatiently
for some late afternoon
in a lost city, in the middle of an unknown country
where i will watch the sun taking its last breaths
while i smile at the idea of that view being my home.

P.S.

sunsets & tangerines

you're great, but

i know i'm too much
i'm sorry but
i can't be less than the whole of me
it's in my blood
i can burn you or i can blind you
with flames as high as skyscrapers
but i could never put out my fire for you
or for anyone else.

P.S.

P.S.

reflection

you put all the energy you got
brooding old ideas
in a reckless attempt to show the world
a face that was never yours
but i knew you
i knew every thought
that slowly crept through your mind
while you thought no one was paying attention
i knew you
and i knew you hated me
'cause you saw in me what you feared most
you saw in my eyes
all the pieces of broken glass
that were held together by a woolen thread
and i knew you were afraid
that i would make all of that collapse on the floor
and you would have to stick them back inside of you
one by one
i knew you
i still know you
more and more with each passing year
but unlike you
i don't run from that gaze anymore
even though i can still see
all shards of glass
shining so defiantly
inside those tired brown eyes.

P.S.

criticism

i know all my flaws by name
all fifty-two of them
i call them every night
between a sip and another of wine
you see, i'm not innocent
i know who i am
and i can read you just fine
so when you highlight all my cracks
trying to forget the things about me
that i know make you gasp for air
it doesn't reach my core
it makes me like me even more.

P.S.

P.S.

chaos theory

i'm made by chaos
you already realized that
and because i'm built by such impulsive forces
i have to carry with me this curse
of changing my feelings every day
just like you change your shoes every week
so you keep looking at me
with heavy eyes and a sad mouth
as if it were my fault that everything is upside down
don't worry, it doesn't hurt me anymore
i understand now why you do this
it's always easier to blame the hurricane
than to place all the blame on a butterfly.

P.S.

to the real me

take a deep breath
really try to feel who you are (just try)
you keep locking yourself in your crystal palace
hiding behind this beautiful facade
even though everything has already crumbled
so try for once to feel yourself
breathe in the dust
that comes from all the broken glass that was left
it's you
stop fighting
and let it be you.

P.S.

P.S.

baby's breath

i spent a long time
believing that
i only had one chance to be happy
so i kept trying so hard
to grow baby's breath
from seeds made of coal
while blaming myself
for not being able
to make grass as fertile as it could be.

P. S.

twenty-eight

i'm getting older
but i have this bad habit
of not wanting to let go of my youth
even though it's letting go of me
with each passing day
today, while i keep looking through big windows
i think about a time
when i could only see the world through small ones
from inside a room
that couldn't contain even the smallest of my dreams
today, i sadly realized
those dreams are long gone
i don't carry bold goals anymore
i lost it, somewhere along the way
today, i know the world
as the imperfect and weak place it is
i thought it would be different after i turned eighteen
i thought it would be different after i graduated
i thought it would be different
it turns out it was, but not in the way i imagined
i have become bitter and conscious of the world
i have become a realistic person
i'm not a dreamer anymore
it's weird, i guess i have no memories
of what i was feeling back then
it's like i was feeling nothing
'til i started to feel it all

P.S.

and now with all these years
pressing my back to the ground
i feel like i'm always overthinking life
that's why i constantly find myself alone
looking at buildings and pouring drinks
sitting on the balcony
like a jukebox with only one song to play
on rainy days like this
when it looks like it hasn't even dawned
i realize why i really am a moonchild
i know i'm doomed to drown in my feelings
and it's not sad
nor happy
it's just what it is
i'm getting older
but i have this bad habit
of not wanting to let go of my youth
even though it's letting go of me
with each passing day
it's just what it is.

P.S.

tangerines

P.S.

coordinates

there is this place

where the air fills you with laughter

and the trees tell you stories about skinned knees

there is this place

that embraces you with the sounds of leaves

and running giggles

and midnight stars' chases

and tastes like tangerines

there is this place

for which you wrote the coordinates

and carefully stored on a piece of skin

like a reminder to yourself

'cause among all the other places

that have marked you with suffering

there is this place

that has marked you with joy and nothing else.

P.S.

the colors of the universe

we thought we could count
all the colors that make up a rainbow
as if it were possible
to lock each one
in a tiny little glass box
oh, darling
the universe has an incredible infinity of colors
which sparkle and dance and explode
with the energy of a million supernovae
you certainly won't be the one who will decide
which one has the real right to shine.

P.S.

P.S.

i would find you

i don't wanna live in a world
where i have never kissed you
played with my fingers along your skin
and felt your hair standing up for me
i don't wanna cross streets
where i have never stepped beside you
while you closed your eyes
to feel the rays of sunlight on your cheeks
i don't wanna visit museums
where i have never met you
sitting and waiting for me
with a smile as big as your heart
and i don't wanna take trains or buses or airplanes
where you have never sat by my side
making jokes about my clumsiness
and laughed at the angry faces i make for others
(but never for you)
i don't wanna do this
i don't wanna live like that
'cause it would be unbearable to live in a world
where my heart is out of my chest.

P.S.

sunsets & tangerines

timezone

when i open my eyes
trying to find a reason to get up
you close yours
praying for a reason to stay strong
but we are both holding the same sheets
wishing for a sign of hope
every time i sit on the balcony
to watch the city wake up for me
you are in a land of dreams
as far as possible from reality
but we are both searching for a purpose
that was painfully lost some time ago
we will always be looking at the same sun
but it will show its light to you
as soon as it leaves me in the darkness
we will always be on opposite sides
but, i know, with the same old doubts
and you will always be like me
and i will always be like you
so remember
when it gets dark and you see fear
i promise i'll be storing strips of light for you
'cause when your morning comes and you can finally breathe
i know you will be catching them for me too.

P.S.

neverland

i picture you singing ballads in the kitchen

while i sip wine with my blue wool sweater

looking out the open window

at the sleepy buildings and the shining lights

of a city that is nowhere to be found

with a life that will never happen

so i smile

feeling all the shivers that a winter day could give me

and i hold on to the windowsill

to leave for a few seconds

just so i can turn off the alarm

just so i can stay a little longer.

P.S.

it scares me

i don't think there will be a time
when i'll look at you
chest up and down
a piece of peace pasted on your face
while your mind is so far away in a land of dreams
and not be terribly afraid (i'm always so terribly afraid)
of a time when there will be no you
when i will fight to keep your smile in my memory
when your roots will be buried in my heart
but i will no longer be able to reach your body
loving you is so fucking scary
'cause loving you makes me want you to stay forever.

P.S.

P.S.

dear mom,

i was thinking what to say to you
you know i don't care about holidays
and i know it hurts you that i don't
but this year i decided that
i needed to give you something
so i wanted to talk about
the parts of you that i remember

first, i remember your hair
which was like mine before
so weak and thin
but it was changed at the exact moment
you decided to carry me in your belly
as if the universe was saying
you had to harden to be a mother
because it would never be easy to deal with me

i remember your eyes too
you know, i have your eyes
the same ones that i always felt were judging me
because they were so hard, all the time
it took me a long while to understand
they were also filled with fear
of what the world would do to me when i was by myself

i also think of your hands
that have carried me over and over
i inherited them from you too
those hard hands
bruised from all the earth you had to move

the same hands that pointed their fingers at me
and then craved so much to hold my body
so i would never leave

i remember your elbows, mom
buried firmly on the table every night
surrounded by so many books
and so many dreams
that you chose to chase
despite the short time
that was given to you

and mostly, i remember your spine
making you stand so upright
with your head up
because you know who you are
and what you did
so you know what you deserve
and you gave me a piece of that pride too
so that i could carry it with me
and use it to hold my chin up, like yours

i know, mom
we have this difficult relationship
i'm not as soft and loving with you as i am with dad
i know it hurts you
but mom, you need to know
it scares me, when i look into your eyes
i can't help being cold
because i see so much of me there
i see so much worry and fear
that i will not be able to be better

P.S.

i see an ocean of love, but mountains of doubt

it's too hard for me to look at you
because it's too hard for me to look at myself
never ever doubt my love for you, mom
because how could i not love
the one that built all the parts of me
saw them shatter on the floor
and even today takes them one by one in her lap
while trying to fit them together tenderly?

P.S.

sunsets & tangerines

two oranges and a spoonful of honey

i know how hard you tried
to make life look like a fairy tale
even if you had to kill dragons
every night lying on your pillow
i know how much you wished
our childhood was perfect and naive
and how you fought to hide us from the world
under fortresses made of sheets
i turned twelve
thinking you were the perfect father
then i went through five more years
saying you were only wrong with me
now i know i will live another fifty
thanking the universe for having given you
the task of making me grow
don't worry, dad
i'll be fine
and my brother will be too
'cause among all the skinned knees
and stories invented to make us sleep
you didn't forget to teach us
that even when it hurts
to the point of crying
we can take two oranges
and a spoonful of honey
put them together
and make tea.

P.S.

P.S.

two beers on the 25th street curb

i remember that night when you first called me crazy
you drank your beer slowly like milk & honey
and said this world was too boring to contain my soul
that i would never stop thinking of things as a waste of time
and there were no trains to the places i needed to go
but then you looked at me
while i was looking at the sky
and said even though you knew
you wouldn't be able to entertain me enough
you wanted so bad to be part of my world
that it would be worth the try.

P.S.

how dare you cross my path

i have a thousand things to do
and yet i can't move
'cause right when i was trying to balance
a cup of coffee
on top of a pile of anxieties
i saw you.

P.S.

P.S.

day one

it started like a startle

and suddenly all my body felt lost for three seconds

then my throat became warm

and i could sense all the emptiness of my stomach

when i realized, i had spoken five words

without any connection between them

so i improvised a silly joke

just to buy time

to understand what the hell was going on with my hands

and then it came

the urge to touch, to feel, to be

so i bit your arm

with the excuse that i always do this with strangers

just to feel you in my mouth

just to find out how it tastes

and when the time to say goodbye came

and you looked at me with those dark beautiful eyes

i forgot right away how it was

how it was to live without your existence

... and i still can't remember.

P.S.

what if the planets had not aligned?

i was looking at you the other night
i always look at you while you sleep
because you know i can't turn off my mind
i have an hour of dreams for every four of you
so i keep looking at you
until my body can't take it and shuts itself down
at that night
i suddenly remembered the day i met you
how completely unpredictable it was
and i found myself wondering
how the universe must have aligned so precisely
for my eyes to meet yours at that very moment
i felt scared
i felt so scared of the possibility
that things would happen differently than they did
of me changing my mind and deciding not to make that trip
of my feet not directing me to the sports court
of my laughter not reaching your ears
and making your eyes search for it
of my mouth not asking you to come back the next day
of my silly jokes not convincing you that i wanted you
of my arms not holding you with enough intention
of my head not turning at the right time when i had to go
of your eyes not realizing in that instant
that i would be yours forever
i was so afraid of each of these moments going wrong
but all i could do was whisper to your dreams
that i would never let you slip through my fingers

P.S.

that i would turn the world upside down
until i found you
and made you mine.

P.S

sunsets & tangerines

remember me

i can't help but wonder
if you are wondering what i'm doing right now
if you are looking at the sky and smiling
at the thought of me watching the sunset with you.

P. S.

P.S.

i'm not afraid of heights (i'm afraid of falling)

you asked me
if i would need to jump off a cliff
into the angry ocean
to know exactly what it feels like
to be free
i answered you
that i would not be free
since i would be carried by the waves
but that i would jump off a cliff
into the angry ocean
if it meant my heart would beat a little faster
then you whispered to the wind
if it wouldn't be easier
to ride a rollercoaster
so my heart could climb my throat
and squeeze it
'til my eyes couldn't keep open
i looked at your lips
and then into your eyes
and said, uneasy
that maybe there were just a few things
that could unsettle me like an angry ocean
and it wasn't a rollercoaster
you wondered what it could be
with a silly blind look on your face
i looked back at the cliff
closed my eyes
listening to the sounds of the waves

so that i had time to control my tongue

so that i had time to slow down my pulse

and said to you

that maybe skydiving

would terrify me.

P.S.

P.S.

men like you

most men don't love

but you do

you devote yourself to it as a religion

you give every single piece of your soul

and every single wanting in your heart

you love

without hesitation or second thoughts

until it consumes you and makes you suffocate

most men don't love

but you do

so i can't help but wish

for a world made by men like you.

P.S.

whisper to me

you love me so quietly
almost in whispers
so subtle that it surprised me
when they said you look at me
like i'm your whole world
you have to understand
why it's so hard for me
i'm used to shouting out loud
all the reasons why i adore you
i'm used to spelling all the letters
that make up your name
like it was candy in my mouth
that's why i didn't realize
that while i was summoning storms
to brighten up your smile
across the dark sky
you were building up a fort
so that the rain wouldn't make me sick.

P.S.

P.S.

memories of a summer

should we do this?

should we go back to that drunk night?

'cause i remember it like it was yesterday

the way the lights colored your skin

you were so pink and then so blue and then so gorgeous

i remember the view

and the sensation of the ice touching my lips

of your hands on my hips and your laughter in my ears

i remember

the feeling of the air running through my hair

when we decided to go see the sea

to feel the sun rising on our skin

and the sand holding onto our feet

i remember you

and i know exactly what you remember about me

you remember my eyes

'cause they never looked so free

as they did at that summer night.

P.S.

sunsets & tangerines

goodbye

i keep repeating to the world

how much i hate you

because you took away my happiness

but you see

now that i have to say goodbye

i can only remember the days

when i wore drunk smiles as big as your skyscrapers

'cause you were my first sip of freedom

and the one that taught me so much

that let me lie down on your tennis courts

watching stars and making wishes

the one who gave me shoulders to cry

despite having created so many tears in me

so i need to thank you for existing in my life

you changed me so much

and it's because of you that today i'm able to say goodbye.

P.S.

real love

real love never dies
it changes
it may look harder
it may look different
it may look prettier
but it never dies.

P.S.

first love

i can remember my first love
she was green and flowery
with countless pages
and smelled like ink
she put together so many pieces of me
that it's hard to remember
how i abandoned her
for months and then years
'til life became so unbearable
that i had to beg her back
so i could breathe again
my first love
came out of my fingers
like serenades
'cause back then
when i first met her
i had not yet known the ugliness of the world
and still believed that if i tried really hard
i could bend the universe
and fly through the sky
my first love
came back to me
like tears and painful silences
salty and deeper and heavier
but as strong as an oak
and it was at that moment that i realized
that even if i force myself to let her go
i will never stop needing her to come back.

P.S.

pride

if one day, who knows, i decide to have children
i will carry a constant fear in my chest
i know i will, so deep it will tear me apart
it will not be a fear of them finding love
it will not be a fear of this love coming from the same gender
it will not be a fear that they would not be strong enough
to withstand the toxicity of society
i will be afraid (so afraid)
to see them stutter
to see their eyes immersed in indecision
wanting to tell me a thousand words
but not knowing where to start
terrified that i will hear them all
with a heart as cold as steel
i will carry a constant fear in my chest
(i know i will)
that i did not show enough love
for them to bring home
those who were lucky enough to win their souls
without feeling the need
to make me sit down and tell me a secret.

P.S.

root

you carry yourself
with the weight of eight generations
and yet so gorgeous
with your callused hands
and watery eyes
tired of the way the world works
but so sweet
like you've never felt on your skin
the cuts of being a woman.

P.S.

one every eight hours

do you know that feeling of getting lost?
of not knowing your surroundings?
of everything being so fresh and new?
it's medicine
just take it and wait fifteen minutes
you're gonna feel better, i promise.

P.S.

sunsets & tangerines

she looks like lilies

she has this kind of feeling
as if the world was not enough to house her heart
and yet she embraces it
with the ferocity of a butterfly
who refuses to believe that she's smaller than a lily
and moves her wings 'til it bends under her storm.

P.S.

P.S.

she gave me comfort

i found her there
when i was touching the borders
of the wildest storm
looking at me with sad eyes
and a warm chest
ready to cover my wounds
with her bare hands
and when we reach each other's arms
without barriers and hesitations
suddenly it felt less lonely
to be in the middle of that hurricane.

P.S.

she doesn't know how to say my name

(but the way she says it warms my heart)

she hugged me

with the tenderness of a home

said to me it would be alright

that it's okay not knowing what you want

told me a handful of stories and adventures

just so i could keep my mind busy

then brought me a cup of tea that smelled like rain

and with all the grace of a flowery dress

she smiled

as if she was going to stay forever.

P.S.

P.S.

forty-one days

for every day of happiness
there are forty ones of cold
i know it's scary
no one wants to be lost
between forty winter days
and forty desert nights
but still
for every forty days of heaviness
there will always be a day to hold.

P.S.

sunsets & tangerines

december, 31

one minute to midnight

and i can hear all the promises leaving strangers' mouths

like chains

attaching themselves to the ground

preventing them from letting go (and giving up)

and among all the pretty colors and loud voices

that fill the heavy houses around me

i see myself

counting minutes whilst i clench my fists

looking for chains that aren't there

and whispering slowly as if asking permission

to make me a promise

that next year i'm gonna try to be happy.

P.S.

Paola M. Sartori

@paolamsartori

Printed in Great Britain
by Amazon